English 1

Practice in the Basic Skills

Contents

Name these things

These start with **a**

These start with **b**

These start with **c**

1 a _ _	**6** b _ _	**11** c _ _
2 a _ _	**7** b _ _ _	**12** c _ _
3 a _ _ _ _	**8** b _ _	**13** c _ _
4 a _ _ _ _ _ _ _	**9** b _ _ _	**14** c _ _
5 a _ _ _ _ _ _	**10** b _ _	**15** c _ _ _ _

bee   apple   cap   bat   anchor   car   ball   ant
camel   cat   bed   acrobat   cup   axe   bus

2

Name these things

1 d _ _

2 d _ _ _

3 d _ _ _

4 e _ _

5 e _ _ _ _ _ _ _

6 f _ _

7 f _ _ _

8 f _ _ _

9 g _ _ _

10 g _ _ _ _ _ _

11 h _ _

12 h _ _

13 h _ _ _

14 h _ _ _ _ _

15 h _ _ _ _ _

girl   hat   garden   dog   egg   hammer   fox   horse
elephant   fire   duck   hand   desk   hen   fish

Name these things

1 i _ _ _ _ _	6 k _ _ _	11 m _ _ _
2 j _ _ _ _	7 l _ _ _	12 m _ _
3 j _ _	8 l _ _ _ _	13 m _ _ _
4 k _ _	9 l _ _ _ _ _	14 n _ _ _
5 k _ _ _	10 l _ _ _	15 n _ _ _

mat	jam	nest	ladder	kite	insect	lamb	moon
lion	jelly	key	lemon	nose	king	milk	

Name these things

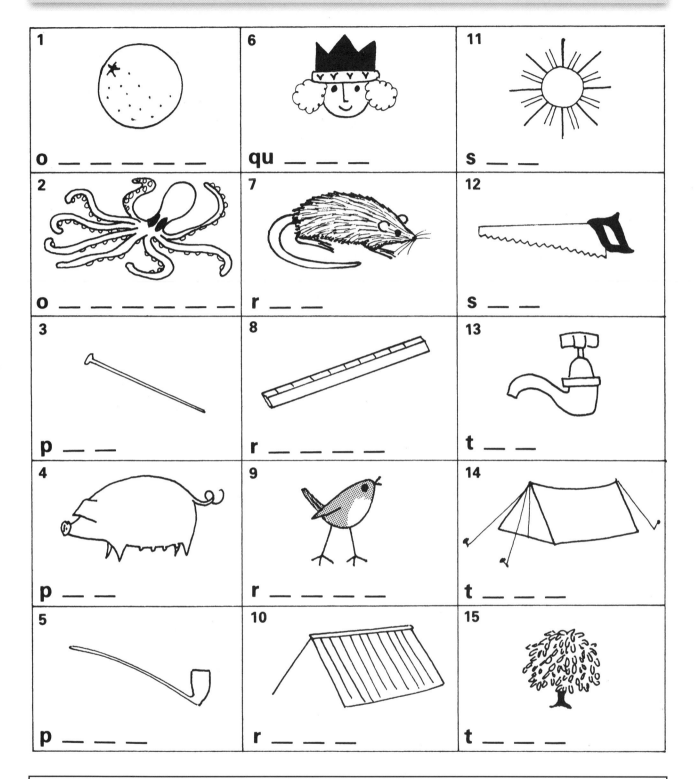

1 o _ _ _ _

2 o _ _ _ _ _ _

3 p _ _

4 p _ _

5 p _ _ _

6 qu _ _ _

7 r _ _

8 r _ _ _ _

9 r _ _ _ _

10 r _ _ _

11 s _ _

12 s _ _

13 t _ _

14 t _ _ _

15 t _ _ _

rat	pipe	queen	tree	orange	pin	robin	sun
tent	pig	octopus	roof	tap	saw	ruler	

Name these things

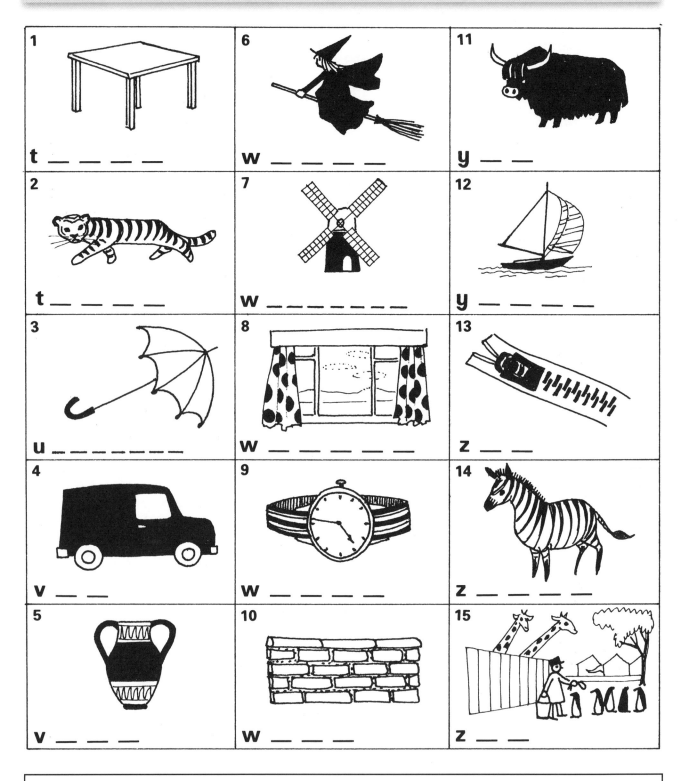

1 t _ _ _ _

2 t _ _ _ _

3 u _ _ _ _ _ _ _ _

4 v _ _ _

5 v _ _ _

6 w _ _ _ _

7 w _ _ _ _ _ _ _

8 w _ _ _ _ _ _

9 w _ _ _ _

10 w _ _ _

11 y _ _

12 y _ _ _ _

13 z _ _

14 z _ _ _ _

15 z _ _

watch	zoo	yak	tiger	witch	zip	table	vase
wall	yacht	van	window	umbrella	zebra	windmill	

First sounds

Write each answer as a word.

1 Which one starts with **b**?

2 Which one starts with **d**?

3 Which one starts with **p**?

4 Which one starts with **b**?

5 Which one starts with **d**?

6 Which one starts with **p**?

7 Which one starts with **b**?

8 Which one starts with **d**?

| book | pan | doll | ball | domino | penny | dart | bed |

Seen at the seaside

Look at the 14 pictures. Each has a number.

Write down what each one is.

The words below will help you.

sandcastle	fish	crab	pebbles	seagull
rocks	yacht	net	speedboat	pier
seaweed	spade	deckchair	cliffs	

Sorting animals

Write the correct animal's name for each picture.

1 camel   **2** ....   **3** ....   **4 and so on.**

These animal names will help you.

rabbit	leopard	dog	pig	sheep	cow
hamster	camel	giraffe	gorilla	hen	cat

Now draw three boxes and label them.

Write the names of the animals in the correct boxes.

home	farm	zoo
		camel

Watch us

Finish these sentences.

1 Watch Lily .... **2** Watch Andrew ....

3 Watch Thomas .... **4** Watch Maki ....

5 Watch Chloe .... **6** Watch Josh ....

| jump | run | climb | swim | skip | slide |

More than one (1)

Look at these pictures.

Finish these sentences.

1   There are three ....

2   There are nine ....

3   There are two ....

4   There are five ....

5   There are four ....

6   There are seven ....

7   There are eight ....

8   There are six ....

stars	**balls**	**cars**	**houses**	**birds**
books	**ladders**	**flowers**		

At home

Look at the picture. 14 things have a number.

Write down what each one is.

The words below will help you.

1 chair   **2** _____   **3** _____   **4 and so on.**

television	settee	window	vase	lamp
chair	curtains	door	radio	carpet
fire	picture	table	books	

Young animals

Now do these.

The words below will help you.

	Mother	→	baby
1	cat	→	__ __ __ __ __ __
2	dog	→	__ __ __ __ __
3	hen	→	__ __ __ __ __ __ __
4	duck	→	__ __ __ __ __ __ __ __
5	cow	→	__ __ __ __
6	horse	→	__ __ __ __
7	sheep	→	__ __ __ __
8	pig	→	__ __ __ __ __ __

kitten	lamb	piglet	puppy
duckling	foal	calf	chicken

13

Ball play

Finish these sentences.

1
Ali can .... the ball.

2
Chloe can .... the ball.

3
Lily can .... the ball.

4
Thomas can .... the ball.

5
Andrew can .... the ball.

6
Maki can .... the ball.

| throw | catch | kick | head | roll | bounce |

Crosswords

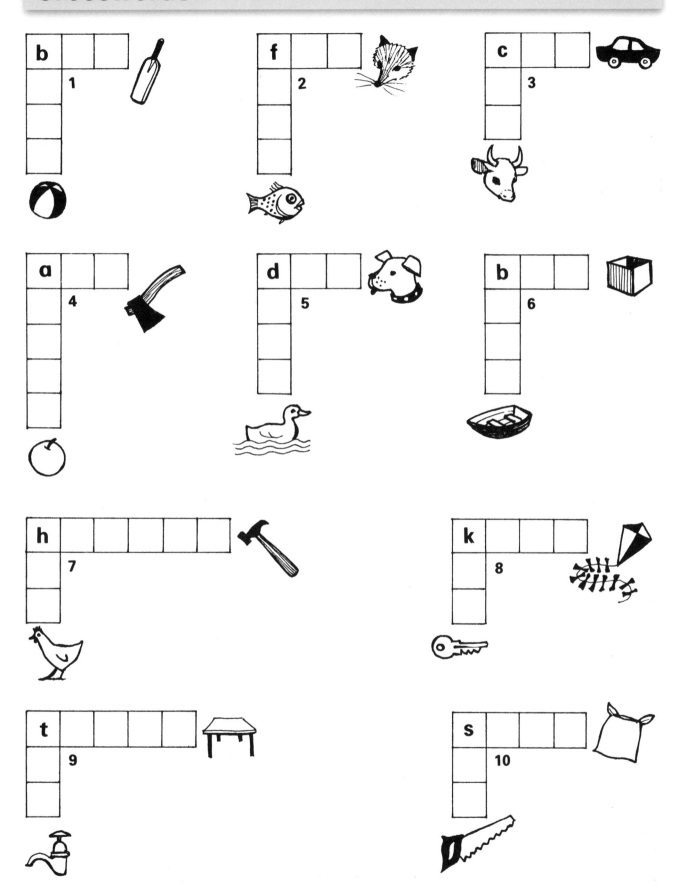

More than one (2)

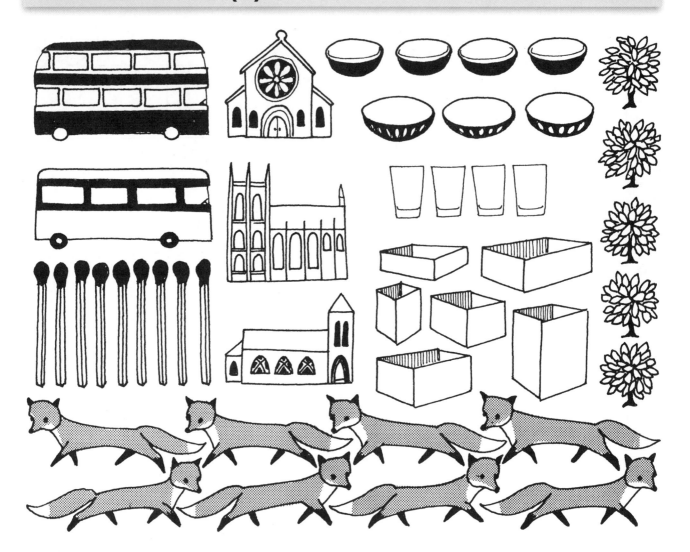

Finish these sentences.

1 There are nine ....

2 There are four ....

3 There are six ....

4 There are three ....

5 There are five ....

6 There are eight ....

7 There are two ....

8 There are seven ....

matches	churches	dishes	boxes
foxes	buses	bushes	glasses

At school

Look at the picture. 14 things have a number.

Write down what each one is.

The words below will help you.

1 balance   **2** .... **and so on.**

easel	sand-tray	books	oven	scissors
aquarium	pencils	milk	sink	brushes
ruler	work-tray	paints	balance	

Animal homes

Where do these animals live?

The words below will help you.

1 A badger → s e t t

2 A dog → ___ ___ ___ ___ ___ ___

3 A bee → ___ ___ ___ ___

4 A horse → ___ ___ ___ ___ ___ ___

5 A rabbit → ___ ___ ___ ___ ___ ___

6 A pig → ___ ___ ___

7 A fox → ___ ___ ___

8 A bird → ___ ___ ___ ___

| nest | hive | sty | burrow | den | stable | sett | kennel |

They are busy

Finish these sentences.

1 Kika likes to _____ .

2 Andrew likes to _____ .

3 Syed likes to _____ .

4 Daisy likes to _____ .

5 Lily likes to _____ .

6 Peter likes to _____ .

| sing | paint | bake | dig | sew | fish |

a in the middle

Fill in the right word.

The pictures and words will help you.

1 We boil eggs in a _____ .

2 I like _____ on my bread.

3 I wear a _____ on my head.

4 I wipe my feet on a _____ .

5 Mum carries shopping in a _____ .

| bag | cap | pan | jam | mat |

e in the middle

10

Fill in the right word.

The pictures and words will help you.

1 The _____ is a useful bird.

2 I sleep in a _____ .

3 Five and five are _____ .

4 I have a right and a left _____ .

5 I write with a _____ .

| pen | ten | leg | bed | hen |

i in the middle

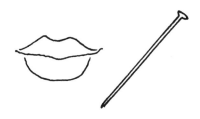   

Fill in the right word.

The pictures and words will help you.

1 A part of your mouth. _____

2 We put litter in a _____ .

3 A _____ has a very sharp point.

4 Baked beans come in a _____ .

5 Some people eat meat from a _____ .

| pig | pin | lip | bin | tin |

o in the middle

Fill in the right word.

The pictures and words will help you.

1 A baby sleeps in a _____ .

2 We clean the floor with a _____ .

3 A thick piece of tree. _____

4 A _____ is a pet.

5 I catch fish with a _____ .

| rod | log | cot | dog | mop |

u in the middle

Fill in the right word.

The pictures and words will help you.

1 A small carpet. _____

2 A farm animal. _____

3 The _____ shines in the sky.

4 I drink out of a _____ .

5 A _____ carries people.

bus	sun	rug	bull	mug

Mixed bag (1)

Fill in the right word.

The pictures and words will help you.

1 A pet. _____

2 See the squirrel eat a _____ .

3 Peas grow in a _____ .

4 A spider makes a _____ .

5 You put rubbish into a _____ .

web	nut	cat	bin	pod

In the park

Look carefully at the picture.

Finish these sentences.

1 .... is coming down the slide.

2 There are .... ducks in the pond.

3 .... is playing with his boat.

4 .... is feeding the swan.

5 .... kicks the ball to ....

6 .... is skipping.

7 .... and .... are on the swings.

8 There are .... trees in the park.

9 .... and .... are on the seesaw.

10 There are .... children in the park.

Word puzzles (1)

Write the words correctly.

   Here is an example   **gba → bag**

These words will help you.

bat	car	mug	bee	web	sun	bed
bus	boy	cat	dog	cow	saw	tap

1   ebe

2   rac

3   was

4   yob

5   ocw

6   tba

7   edb

8   gdo

9   tac

10   snu

11   gum

12   sbu

13   pat

14   bew

Animal sounds

Find the correct sounds.

The words below will help you.

1 A cat ___ ___ ___ ___ ___.

2 A dog ___ ___ ___ ___ .

3 A pig ___ ___ ___ ___ ___ .

4 A duck ___ ___ ___ ___ ___ ___ .

5 A lion ___ ___ ___ ___ ___ .

6 An owl ___ ___ ___ ___ ___ .

7 A lamb ___ ___ ___ ___ ___ ___ .

8 A monkey ___ ___ ___ ___ ___ ___ ___ ___ .

purrs	**roars**	**chatters**	**bleats**
hoots	**barks**	**quacks**	**grunts**

oo in the middle

1 b _ _ _

2 h _ _ _

3 b _ _ _

4 p _ _ _

5 g _ _ _ _

6 r _ _ _

7 r _ _ _

8 r _ _ _

9 s _ _ _ _

10 b _ _ _ _ _

11 h _ _ _

12 b _ _ _ _

goose	stool	root	book	boot	broom
rook	pool	brook	roof	hoop	hook

26

Rhymes (1)

Which word has the same sound as the word in bold type?

Write your answers like this:

1   man   can

2   cap   .... **and so on.**

1	**man**	may	mat	can	run
2	**cap**	car	tap	lot	cat
3	**mat**	cat	bed	man	may
4	**bed**	boy	fin	bad	red
5	**pen**	leg	log	ten	pig
6	**net**	pet	not	put	mat
7	**nib**	rid	nip	bin	rib
8	**lid**	lit	kid	dim	lip
9	**pig**	wig	tip	pot	pad
10	**lip**	kit	hid	dip	tin
11	**pin**	bit	fin	pip	tip
12	**rod**	hop	cot	fog	pod
13	**log**	mop	dog	pot	rob
14	**mop**	dot	nod	top	cot
15	**cot**	dot	cod	dog	top
16	**bud**	bus	cub	sum	mud
17	**rug**	mug	gum	tub	rub
18	**sun**	nut	tug	bun	bud
19	**cup**	bun	pup	cub	bus
20	**hut**	hub	fun	mum	nut

Choose the right word

Look at each picture carefully.

Write out the correct word for the picture like this:

1 plaice   **2** .... **, and so on.**

1 plaice plate place	**2** aunt and ant	**3** boy buoy buy
4 beer bear bare	**5** beech beach bench	**6** quay key kerb
7 pale pail paid	**8** sea say see	**9** rose rows nose
10 flour floor flower	**11** wood would world	**12** pair pear pare

Double letters

Many words have double letters, like apple and book.

Write out the correct word for the picture like this:

1   apple   2 .... **, and so on.**

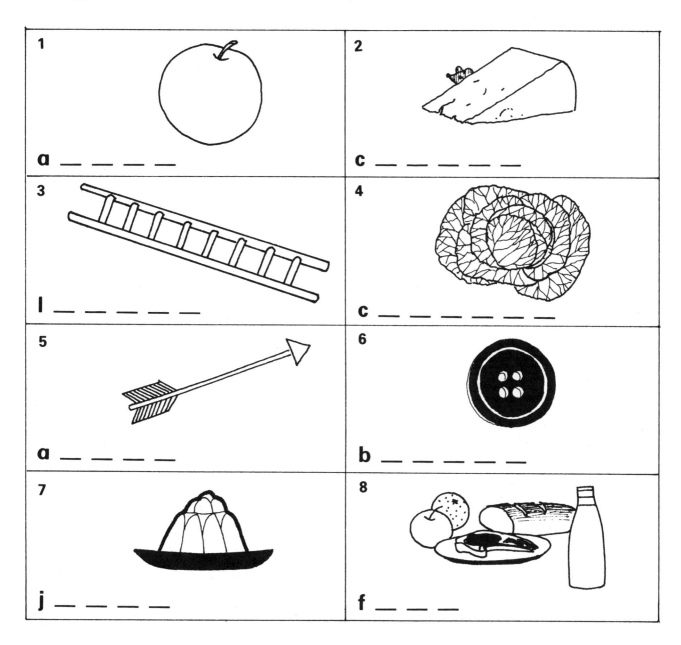

1 a _ _ _ _	2 c _ _ _ _ _
3 l _ _ _ _ _	**4** c _ _ _ _ _ _
5 a _ _ _ _	**6** b _ _ _ _ _
7 j _ _ _ _	**8** f _ _ _

ladder	button	jelly	cheese
apple	food	cabbage	arrow

People at work

Who does which job?

The words below will help you.

1 The __ __ __ __ __ __ __ looks after our teeth.

2 The __ __ __ __ __ __ __ __ puts out fires.

3 The __ __ __ __ __ works in a hospital.

4 The __ __ __ __ __ flies aeroplanes.

5 The __ __ __ __ __ __ __ sells meat.

6 The __ __ __ cares for animals.

7 The __ __ __ __ __ makes bread and cakes.

8 The __ __ __ __ __ __ __ brings our letters.

dentist	pilot	butcher	vet
baker	postman	nurse	firefighter

Word puzzles (2)

Write the words correctly.

Here is an example   **olin → lion**

These words will help you.

moon	king	book	nail	boat	tree	bird
leaf	duck	fish	girl	loaf	foot	goat

1   abot

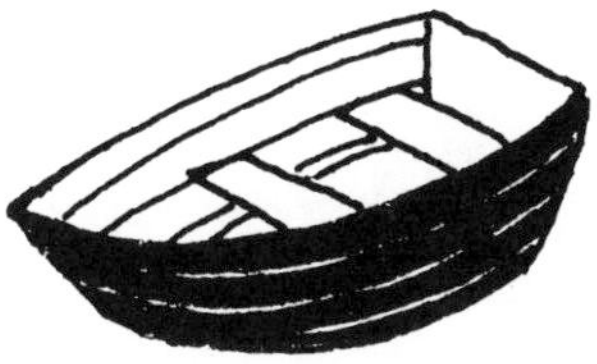

2   drib

3   shif

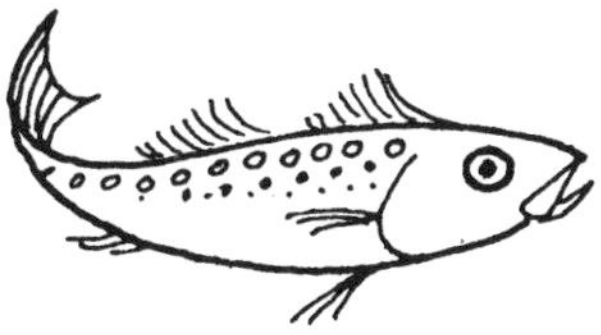

4   lirg

5   aefl

6   onom

7   otof

8   olaf

9   kobo

10   rete

11   tgao

12   cudk

13   lian

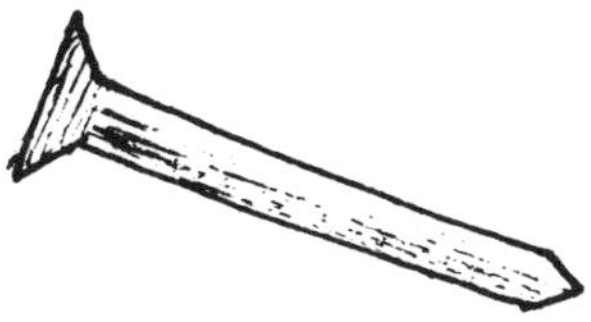

14   ignk

Crosswords

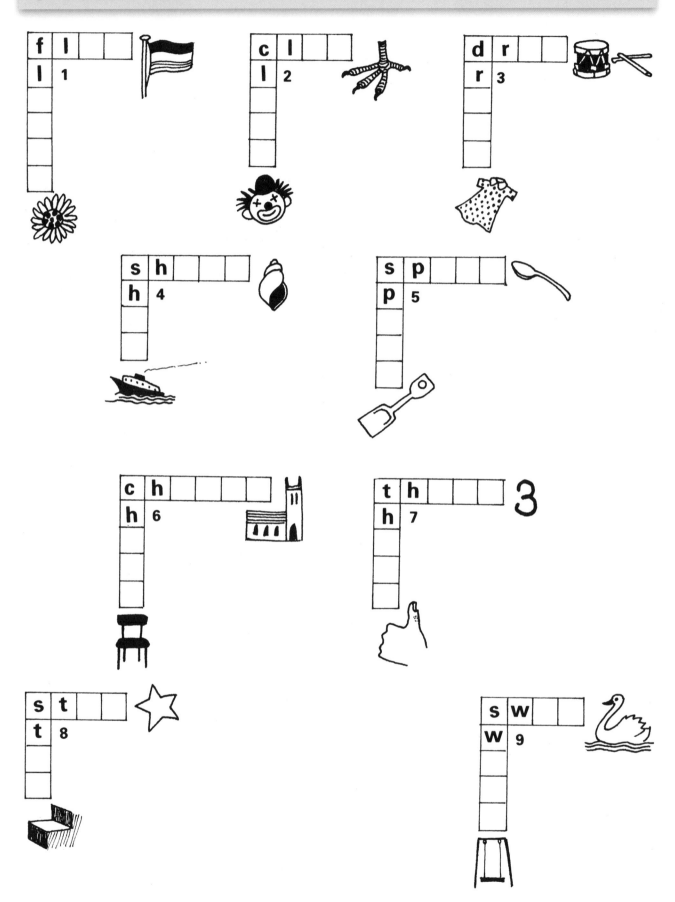

Completing sentences

A These sentences have been divided, but the halves are not in the right order.

Write out the correct sentences.

1	The gorilla ...	swam away.
2	Birds ...	has a roof.
3	The fish ...	scored a goal.
4	The airliner ...	was in the zoo.
5	Mark ...	landed at the airport.
6	A house ...	have feathers.

B A word has been left out of these sentences.

Choose the right word from the brackets to complete the sentences.

The first one has been done for you.

1 Tom **shuts** the door.   (shuts, bends, sleeps)

2 The dog _____ his tail.   (sits, wags, runs)

3 The farmer _____ the cow.   (runs, looks, milks)

4 Chen-Wu _____ into the mirror.   (lifts, looks, digs)

5 The postman _____ the letters.   (builds, feeds, brings)

6 Dad _____ his motor car.   (drives, bakes, writes)

7 Mariam _____ her bicycle.   (reads, rides, barks)

8 Mum _____ the clothes.   (paints, writes, washes)

9 Mark always _____ his teeth every day.   (writes, brushes, sits)

10 The baby _____ in the pram.   (runs, sleeps, writes)

What are they?

Fill in the correct word.

These words will help you.

numbers	months	tools	fruits	boys
flowers	letters	birds	seasons	fish

1 Apples and oranges are ....

2 Winter and summer are ....

3 Robin and thrush are ....

4 Six and nine are ....

5 Cod and herring are ....

6 January and July are ....

7 D and F are ....

8 Hammer and saw are ....

9 Paul and Mark are ....

10 Daisy and buttercup are ....

Words that begin with ch

Choose the right word.

The words below will help you.

1 Fish and _____ .

2 I use _____ to write on the blackboard.

3 Some people get married in _____ .

4 A young girl or boy. _____

5 A large, strong box. _____

6 I sit on a _____ .

chest	church	chair	chips	chalk	child

Words that end with ch

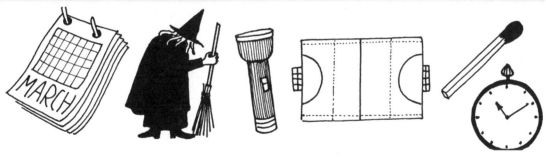

1 A _____ helps you to see in the dark.

2 We play football on a _____ .

3 _____ is the third month of the year.

4 I tell the time with a _____ .

5 A _____ has a broomstick.

6 You can use a _____ to start a fire.

pitch	witch	watch	March	torch	match

Colours

brown	silver	blue	white	green	red	yellow	black

Complete these sentences. Choose the correct colour from the list above.

1 A buttercup is _____ .

2 Snow is _____ .

3 Grass is _____ .

4 Chocolate is _____ .

5 Coal is _____ .

6 The moon is _____ .

7 A pillar box is _____ .

8 The sky is _____ .

Opposites

weak	empty	straight	new	fast
quiet	dirty	hard	early	wet

Write the opposite of the word in bold type, choosing from the list above.

1 My book is **old**, but yours is _____ .

2 Oliver was **late** for school, but Clare was _____ .

3 David is a **slow** worker, but Paul is _____ .

4 The elephant is **strong**, but the mouse is _____ .

5 My toffee is **soft**, but yours is _____ .

6 Your hands are **dry**, but mine are _____ .

7 This room is _____ , but that room is **noisy**.

8 I have a **full** bottle of water, but yours is _____ .

9 The corridor is _____ , but the hall is **clean**.

10 That line is **bent**, while that one is _____ .

Rhymes (2)

Which word has the same sound as the word in bold type?

Write your answers like this:

1   **fly**   cry   **2**   **bread**   .... , and so on.

1	**fly**	cry	two	may	flop
2	**bread**	bead	bear	head	bored
3	**rain**	rail	train	ran	wait
4	**tray**	toy	try	door	day
5	**sail**	nail	fall	soil	foil
6	**neat**	near	more	meat	need
7	**soon**	sort	moon	soot	sun
8	**glow**	blue	group	groan	blow
9	**joy**	toy	top	jam	bow
10	**cow**	cap	cut	now	grow
11	**nose**	must	rose	news	noise
12	**glue**	glad	blow	glum	blue
13	**late**	lame	hate	lane	lake
14	**gold**	held	gulp	grab	sold
15	**son**	sun	saw	burn	some
16	**bare**	bore	fair	bead	bow
17	**stain**	stair	stone	lane	blame
18	**made**	maid	male	mare	make
19	**word**	board	ward	bird	work
20	**their**	thin	there	them	those

is or are

Complete the sentences using **is** or **are**.

1   The dog _____ in the field.

2   The dogs _____ in the field.

3   The cup _____ on the table.

4   Jameela _____ my sister.

5   The lemons _____ sour.

6   _____ this your coat?

7   Tim and David _____ over there.

8   There _____ my house.

9   _____ these your books?

10   Kittens _____ playful.

was or were

Complete the sentences using **was** or **were**.

1   The bus _____ late.

2   The bread _____ stale.

3   The apples _____ sweet.

4   Sophie _____ skipping.

5   The girls _____ in the park.

6   _____ your book exciting?

7   Connor and Heather _____ early for school.

8   The cows _____ in the field.

9   The buses _____ late.

10   _____ you at the football match?

Who's who?

Fill in the correct word.

pilot	dentist	firefighter	nurse
farmer	miner	fisherman	vet

1 He works under the ground.

He gets out coal.

He is a _____ .

2 He works in the fields.

He grows crops and keeps animals.

He is a _____ .

3 She looks after people who are ill.

Often she works in a hospital.

She is a _____ .

4 He cares for sick animals.

He is a _____ .

5 He works on a boat.

He uses a net.

He is a _____ .

6 She looks after your teeth.

She is a _____ .

7 He is often in the air.

He travels quickly.

He is a _____ .

8 She wears a helmet.

She is brave.

She is a _____ .

Jumbled sentences

Arrange the following words to make sentences.

1 goal Mark a scored

2 finger cut Ian his

3 licks cat her The paw

4 pond Kate the into fell

5 the Dad lawn cuts

6 lit Heather bonfire the

7 a Ahmed letter posted

8 gate The over horse the jumped

a or an

Write **a** or **an** before each of the following words.

1 .... cup

2 .... apple

3 .... donkey

4 .... leg

5 .... orange

6 .... ear

7 .... nose

8 .... horse

9 .... arm

10 .... girl

11 .... umbrella

12 .... owl

13 .... desk

14 .... hen

15 .... island

Complete the sentences using **a** or **an**.

1 Mum gave me .... orange.

2 A mouse is smaller than .... elephant.

3 Kim bought .... ice cream.

4 Paul wore .... anorak.

5 Amelia found .... umbrella.

6 David gave Peter .... football.

7 Dad sat in .... armchair and read .... book.

8 A bird built .... nest in .... oak tree.

9 Sam ate .... apple and .... pear.

10 Sometimes .... Eskimo lives in .... igloo.

By the seaside

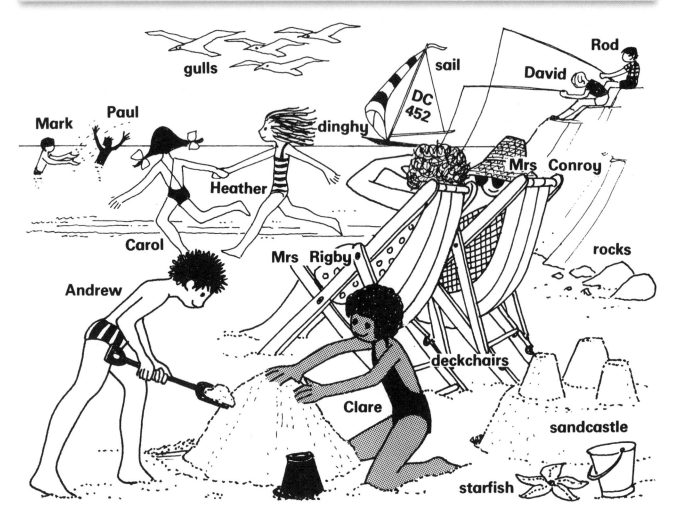

Look carefully at the picture.

Finish these sentences.

1 There are .... gulls flying in the sky.

2 .... and .... are fishing from the rocks.

3 .... and .... are splashing in the sea.

4 .... and .... are running to the sea.

5 .... and .... are making a sandcastle.

6 A .... is near the sandcastle.

7 .... and .... are in the deckchairs.

8 I can read .... on the sail of the dinghy.

Choosing words

A   Pick out six foods.

eggs	matches	bread	pebbles
sticks	coal	string	apples
pans	chicken	books	bottles
onions	spoons	cakes	watches

B   Pick out six things we see on a farm.

fields	lions	plough	barn
soldiers	cows	parrots	train
hens	planes	ship	elephant
igloos	shop	tractor	rocket

C   Pick out six things we wear.

boots	books	stairs	jackets
tools	shoes	jeans	bricks
shirts	cups	boxes	rugs
mirrors	pencils	fields	skirts

D   Pick out six things that travel on roads.

buses	ships	castles	bicycles
planes	motorbikes	books	houses
helicopters	schools	forests	taxis
lorries	yachts	cars	boats

Find the best word

Complete the following sentences by choosing the best word from the list.

A

cruel	brave	blind	heavy	busy

1   The .... man kicked the puppy.

2   A .... man cannot see.

3   The .... firefighter rescued the lady from the fire.

4   Tom found the box too .... to lift.

5   Christmas is a .... time in the shops.

B

sharp	sour	steep	loud	sweet

1   The mountain was too .... to climb.

2   Sugar is ....

3   Adam cut his finger on a .... knife.

4   The firework made a .... noise.

5   The lemon was ....

C

unhappy	fierce	dirty	difficult	bright

1   The wildcat is a .... animal.

2   Sally cried because she was ....

3   Amelia could not see because the sun was ....

4   John was .... after he fell in the mud.

5   The puzzle was too .... for Jake to finish.

The best word

Complete the following sentences by choosing the best word from the list.

A

banged	blew	ate	swam	asked

1 The rabbit _____ two carrots.

2 The fish _____ under the weeds.

3 Gary _____ his drum.

4 Mary _____ me to go for a walk.

5 The strong wind _____ down the tree.

B

chased	drank	crawled	flew	marched

1 The soldiers _____ along the road.

2 Gemma was so thirsty she _____ two bottles of water.

3 The aeroplane _____ from London to Paris.

4 The dog _____ the cat out of the garden.

5 Jenny _____ under the hedge for the ball.

C

whispered	baked	climbed	bought	cheered

1 Dad _____ a new lawnmower.

2 We _____ when Darren scored a goal.

3 Nicola _____ so softly I could not hear her.

4 The cat _____ up the tall tree.

5 My mum _____ a cake for our School Fair.

Writing sentences

Add words of your own to make good sentences.
The pictures will help you.

1   The farmer

2   Shazia buys

3   The elephant

4   The astronaut

5   The painter

6   The ship

7   Grace

8   The train

9   The monkeys

10 The boys

Mixed bag (2)

A Write out the two words that mean the same.

For example: **halt**   run   **stop**   hop

1	fall	lift	drop	push
2	start	begin	end	carry
3	huge	little	small	circle
4	ocean	beach	cliff	sea
5	fast	slow	quick	stop

B Write out these words in order of size.

Begin with the largest.

For example:

cat   elephant   mouse   →   **elephant**   **cat**   **mouse**

1	page	word	book
2	tree	branch	leaf
3	ten	six	one
4	week	year	day
5	frog	giraffe	dog

C Which is always wet?

For example: brush   **rain**   bucket   spade

1	cakes	pies	lemonade	bread
2	grass	trees	flowers	pond
3	lake	hill	mountain	path
4	bridge	river	lane	road
5	cliffs	sand	rock	sea

Mixed bag

A Make a new word using the same letters.

1 gum $\rightarrow$ _(mug)_

2 rats $\rightarrow$ _(star)_

3 reap $\rightarrow$ _(pear)_

4 tools $\rightarrow$ _(stool)_

5 hips $\rightarrow$ _(ship)_

B Write out the opposite of these words.

Choose from this list.

sell	empty	dirty	last	soft	odd	awake	shut

1 even ....

2 clean ....

3 buy ....

4 open ....

5 hard ....

6 asleep ....

7 full ....

8 first ....

C Write out the correct answer.

1 Which is not a flower?   (snowdrop, rose, buttercup, lettuce)

2 Which is not a fish?   (salmon, duck, pike, herring)

3 Which is not a bird?   (thrush, robin, fly, gull)

4 Which is not a tree?   (ash, pine, oak, grass)

5 Which is not a colour?   (yellow, down, green, red)

6 Which is not a fruit?   (apple, pair, orange, banana)

7 Which is not a food?   (bread, biscuit, plate, cake)

8 Which is not a boy's name?   (David, Jack, Jane, Liam)

Answers

Page 2 Name these things
1 ant **2** axe **3** apple **4** acrobat **5** anchor **6** bat
7 bus **8** bee **9** ball **10** bed **11** cat **12** cap
13 car **14** cup **15** camel

Page 3 Name these things
1 dog **2** duck **3** desk **4** egg **5** elephant **6** fox
7 fish **8** fire **9** girl **10** garden **11** hen **12** hat
13 hand **14** horse **15** hammer

Page 4 Name these things
1 insect **2** jelly **3** jam **4** key **5** king **6** kite **7** lion
8 lemon **9** ladder **10** lamb **11** milk **12** mat
13 moon **14** nose **15** nest

Page 5 Name these things
1 orange **2** octopus **3** pin **4** pig **5** pipe **6** queen
7 rat **8** ruler **9** robin **10** roof **11** sun **12** saw
13 tap **14** tent **15** tree

Page 6 Name these things
1 table **2** tiger **3** umbrella **4** van **5** vase **6** witch
7 windmill **8** window **9** watch **10** wall **11** yak
12 yacht **13** zip **14** zebra **15** zoo

Page 7 First sounds
1 ball **2** dart **3** pan **4** bed **5** domino **6** penny
7 book **8** doll

Page 8 Seen at the seaside
1 pier **2** sandcastle **3** yacht **4** cliffs **5** spade
6 seaweed **7** crab **8** rocks **9** deckchair **10** seagull
11 speedboat **12** fish **13** pebbles **14** net

Page 9 Sorting animals
1 camel **2** dog **3** cow **4** rabbit **5** giraffe **6** cat
7 sheep **8** hen **9** pig **10** gorilla **11** leopard
12 hamster
home dog, cat, rabbit, hamster
farm cow, hen, sheep, pig
zoo camel, giraffe, gorilla, leopard

Page 10 Watch us
1 skip **2** climb **3** jump **4** slide **5** run **6** swim

Page 11 More than one (1)
1 ladders **2** balls **3** houses **4** birds **5** cars
6 books **7** stars **8** flowers

Page 12 At home
1 chair **2** television **3** carpet **4** picture **5** vase
6 books **7** settee **8** lamp **9** curtains **10** window
11 table **12** door **13** radio **14** fire

Page 13 Young animals
1 kitten **2** puppy **3** chicken **4** duckling **5** calf
6 foal **7** lamb **8** piglet

Page 14 Ball play
1 head **2** throw **3** roll **4** kick **5** catch **6** bounce

Page 15 Crosswords
1 bat, ball **2** fox, fish **3** car, cow **4** axe, apple
5 dog, duck **6** box, boat **7** hammer, hen
8 kite, key **9** table, tap **10** sack, saw

Page 16 More than one (2)
1 matches **2** glasses **3** boxes **4** churches **5** bushes
6 foxes **7** buses **8** dishes

Page 17 At school
1 balance **2** milk **3** paints **4** aquarium **5** books
6 brushes **7** sand-tray **8** scissors **9** oven **10** ruler
11 work-tray **12** pencils **13** sink **14** easel

Page 18 Animal homes
1 sett **2** kennel **3** hive **4** stable **5** burrow **6** sty
7 den **8** nest

Page 19 They are busy
1 sew **2** paint **3** fish **4** bake **5** sing **6** dig

Page 20 a in the middle
1 pan **2** jam **3** cap **4** mat **5** bag

e in the middle
1 hen **2** bed **3** ten **4** leg **5** pen

Page 21 i in the middle
1 lip **2** bin **3** pin **4** tin **5** pig

o in the middle
1 cot **2** mop **3** log **4** dog **5** rod

Page 22 u in the middle
1 rug **2** bull **3** sun **4** mug **5** bus

Mixed bag
1 cat **2** nut **3** pod **4** web **5** bin

Page 23 In the park
1 John **2** three **3** Andy **4** Susan **5** Rod, Mark
6 Sally **7** Cathy, Andrew **8** seven **9** Jill, Gary **10** ten

Page 24 Word puzzle (1)
1 bee **2** car **3** saw **4** boy **5** cow **6** bat **7** bed **8** dog **9** cat
10 sun **11** mug **12** bus **13** tap **14** web

Page 25 Animal sounds
1 purrs **2** barks **3** grunts **4** quacks **5** roars **6** hoots
7 bleats **8** chatters

Page 26 oo in the middle
1 book **2** hook **3** boot **4** pool **5** goose **6** rook **7** root **8** roof
9 stool **10** broom **11** hoop **12** brook

Page 27 Rhymes (1)
1 can **2** tap **3** cat **4** red **5** ten **6** pet **7** rib **8** kid **9** wig
10 dip **11** fin **12** pod **13** dog **14** top **15** dot **16** mud
17 mug **18** bun **19** pup **20** nut

Page 28 Choose the right word
1 plaice **2** ant **3** buoy **4** bear **5** beach **6** key **7** pail **8** sea
9 rose **10** flower **11** wood **12** pear

Page 29 Double letters
1 apple **2** cheese **3** ladder **4** cabbage **5** arrow **6** button
7 jelly **8** food

Page 30 People at work
1 dentist **2** firefighter **3** nurse **4** pilot **5** butcher **6** vet **7** baker
8 postman

Page 31 Word puzzles (2)
1 boat **2** bird **3** fish **4** girl **5** leaf **6** moon **7** foot **8** loaf
9 book **10** tree **11** goat **12** duck **13** nail **14** king

Page 32 Crosswords
1 flag, flower **2** claw, clown **3** drum, dress **4** shell, ship
5 spoon, spade **6** church, chair **7** three, thumb **8** star, step
9 swan, swing

Page 33 Completing sentences
A 1 The gorilla was in the zoo. **2** Birds have feathers.
3 The fish swam away. **4** The airliner landed at the airport.
5 Mark scored a goal. **6** A house has a roof.
B 1 shuts **2** wags **3** milks **4** looks **5** brings **6** drives **7** rides
8 washes **9** brushes **10** sleeps

Page 34 What are they?
1 fruits **2** seasons **3** birds **4** numbers **5** fish **6** months
7 letters **8** tools **9** boys **10** flowers

Page 35 Words that begin with ch
1 chips 2 chalk 3 church 4 child 5 chest 6 chair

Words that end with ch
1 torch 2 pitch 3 March 4 watch 5 witch 6 match

Page 36 Colours
1 yellow 2 white 3 green 4 brown 5 black 6 silver 7 red
8 blue

Opposites
1 new 2 early 3 fast 4 weak 5 hard 6 wet 7 quiet 8 empty
9 dirty 10 straight

Page 37 Rhymes (2)
1 cry 2 head 3 train 4 day 5 nail 6 meat 7 moon 8 blow
9 toy 10 now 11 rose 12 blue 13 hate 14 sold 15 sun
16 fair 17 lane 18 maid 19 bird 20 there

Page 38 is or are
1 is 2 are 3 is 4 is 5 are 6 Is 7 are 8 is 9 Are 10 are

was or were
1 was 2 was 3 were 4 was 5 were 6 Was 7 were 8 were
9 were 10 Were

Page 39 Who's who?
1 miner 2 farmer 3 nurse 4 vet 5 fisherman 6 dentist
7 pilot 8 firefighter

Page 40 Jumbled sentences
1 Mark scored a goal. **2** Ian cut his finger. **3** The cat licks her paw. **4** Kate fell into the pond. **5** Dad cuts the lawn.
6 Heather lit the bonfire. **7** Ahmed posted a letter.
8 The horse jumped over the gate.

Page 41 a and an
1 a **2** an **3** a **4** a **5** an **6** an **7** a **8** a **9** an **10** a **11** an
12 an **13** a **14** a **15** an
1 an **2** an **3** an **4** an **5** an **6** a **7** an, a **8** a, an **9** an, a
10 an, an

Page 42 By the seaside
1 four **2** David, Rod **3** Mark, Paul **4** Carol, Heather
5 Andrew, Clare **6** starfish **7** Mrs Rigby, Mrs Conroy
8 DC 452

Page 43 Choosing words
A eggs, bread, apples, chicken, onions, cakes
B fields, plough, barn, cows, hens, tractor
C boots, jackets, shoes, jeans, shirts, skirts
D buses, bicycles, motorbikes, taxis, lorries, cars

Page 44 Find the best word
A 1 cruel **2** blind **3** brave **4** heavy **5** busy
B 1 steep **2** sweet **3** sharp **4** loud **5** sour
C 1 fierce **2** unhappy **3** bright **4** dirty **5** difficult

Page 45 The best word
A 1 ate **2** swam **3** banged **4** asked **5** blew
B 1 marched **2** drank **3** flew **4** chased **5** crawled
C 1 bought **2** cheered **3** whispered **4** climbed **5** baked

Page 46 Writing sentences

1–10 Check that your child's sentences describe the matching pictures.

Page 47 Mixed bag

A 1 fall, drop **2** start, begin **3** little, small **4** ocean, sea **5** fast, quick

B 1 book, page, word **2** tree, branch, leaf **3** ten, six, one **4** year, week, day **5** giraffe, dog, frog

C 1 lemonade **2** pond **3** lake **4** river **5** sea

Page 48 Mixed bag

A 1 mug **2** star **3** pear **4** stool **5** ship

B 1 odd **2** dirty **3** sell **4** shut **5** soft **6** awake **7** empty **8** last

C 1 lettuce **2** duck **3** fly **4** grass **5** down **6** pair **7** plate **8** Jane

Published by Collins
An imprint of HarperCollins*Publishers* Ltd
1 London Bridge Street
London
SE1 9GF

Browse the complete Collins catalogue at
www.collins.co.uk

First published in 1978
This edition first published in 2012

© Derek Newton and David Smith 2012

10 9 8 7 6 5

ISBN 978-0-00-750542-5

British Library Cataloguing in Publication Data.
A catalogue record for this publication is available from the British Library.

Project managed by Katie Galloway
Production by Rebecca Evans
Page layout by Exemplarr Worldwide Ltd
Illustrated by A. Rodger
Printed in China

MIX
Paper from
responsible sources
FSC www.fsc.org **FSC™ C007454**

FSC™ is a non-profit international organisation established to promote the responsible management of the world's forests. Products carrying the FSC label are independently certified to assure consumers that they come from forests that are managed to meet the social, economic and ecological needs of present and future generations, and other controlled sources.

Find out more about HarperCollins and the environment at
www.harpercollins.co.uk/green